Super Giggles

Knock-Knocks, Jokes, and Tongue-Twisters

BARNES & NOBLE BOOKS

NEW YORK

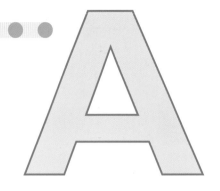

Knock-Knock.
　Who's there?
A-1.
　A-1 who?
A-1 to know.

Knock-Knock.
　Who's there?
Abner.
　Abner who?
Abner-cadabra!

Knock-Knock.
　Who's there?
Alfie.
　Alfie who?
Alfie you later!

Knock-Knock.
  Who's there?
Alibi.
  Alibi who?
Alibi you ice cream.

Knock-Knock.
  Who's there?
Alistair.
  Alistair who?
**Alistair at the TV until
I fall asleep.**

Knock-Knock.
  Who's there?
Alfreda.
  Alfreda who?
Alfreda the dark.

Knock-Knock.
　Who's there?
Alpha.
　Alpha who?
Alpha one and one for all!

Knock-Knock.
　Who's there?
Amarillo.
　Amarillo who?
Amarillo fashioned girl.

Knock-Knock.
　Who's there?
Amusing.
　Amusing who?
Amusing the phone right now.

Knock-Knock.
 Who's there?
Bacon.
 Bacon who?
Bacon your pardon.

Knock-Knock.
 Who's there?
Beacon.
 Beacon who?
Beacon and eggs for breakfast.

Knock-Knock.
 Who's there?
Beagles.
 Beagles who?
Beagles and cream cheese.

Knock-Knock.
 Who's there?
Beach.
 Beach who?
Knock-Knock.
 Who's there?
Beach.
 Beach who?
Knock-Knock.
 Who's there?
Beach.
 Beach who?
Knock-Knock.
 Who's there?
Shore.
 Shore who?
**Shore glad I didn't say
Beach again, aren't you?**

Knock-Knock.
  Who's there?
Beets.
  Beets who?
Beets me. I forgot my name.

Knock-Knock.
  Who's there?
Bella.
  Bella who?
Bella the door isn't working.

Knock-Knock.
  Who's there?
Ben.
  Ben who?
Ben knocking so long my hand hurts.

Knock-Knock.
  Who's there?
Ben and Don.
  Ben and Don who?
Ben there, Don that.

Knock-Knock.
  Who's there?
Beth.
  Beth who?
Beth you can't guess.

Knock-Knock.
  Who's there?
Bess.
  Bess who?
Bess of luck.

Knock-Knock.
  Who's there?
Blast.
  Blast who?
Blast chance to open the door!

C

Knock-Knock.
Who's there?
Canoe.
Canoe who?
Canoe help me with my homework?

Knock-Knock.
Who's there?
Cargo.
Cargo who?
Cargo "Vroom, vroom!"

Knock-Knock.
Who's there?
Cattle.
Cattle who?
Cattle screech if you step on its tail.

Knock-Knock.
  Who's there?
Colleen.
  Colleen who?
Colleen up your room.

Knock-Knock.
  Who's there?
Chicken.
  Chicken who?
Chicken up on you.

Knock-Knock.
  Who's there?
Cohen.
  Cohen who?
Cohen around in circles.

Knock-Knock.
  Who's there?
Clark Kent.
  Clark Kent who?
**Clark Kent come,
he's sick.**

Knock-Knock.
Who's there?
Denise.
Denise who?
Denise is de sister of de nephew.

Knock-Knock.
Who's there?
Dewey.
Dewey who?
Dewey have to wait out here all day?

Knock-Knock.
Who's there?
Dinosaur.
Dinosaur who?
Dinosaur because he stubbed his toe.

Knock-Knock.
  Who's there?
Doug.
  Doug who?
Doug a hole on your doorstep.

Knock-Knock.
  Who's there?
Donna.
  Donna who?
Donna tell me it's bedtime!

Knock-Knock.
  Who's there?
Dots.
  Dots who?
Dots for me to know and you to find out.

Knock-Knock.
  Who's there?
E.T.
  E.T. who?
**E.T. your food
before it gets cold.**

Knock-Knock.
  Who's there?
Event.
  Event who?
Event that-a-way.

Knock-Knock.
  Who's there?
Emil.
  Emil who?
Emil fit for a king.

Knock-Knock.
   Who's there?
Furs.
   Furs who?
Furs come first served.

Knock-Knock.
   Who's there?
Flossie.
   Flossie who?
Flossie your teeth.

Knock-Knock.
   Who's there?
Fletcher.
   Fletcher who?
Fletcher hair down.

Knock-Knock
Who's there?
Gladys.
Gladys who?
Gladys Friday!

Knock-Knock
Who's there?
Gnome.
Gnome who?
Gnome sweet gnome!

Knock-Knock.
Who's there?
Gwen.
Gwen who?
Gwen it rains it pours.

Knock-Knock.
Who's there?
Gruesome.
Gruesome who?
Gruesome tomatoes in my garden.

18

Knock-Knock.
  Who's there?
Habit.
  Habit who?
Habit your way.

Knock-Knock.
  Who's there?
Hannah.
  Hannah who?
Hannah me some bubble gum.

Knock-Knock.
  Who's there?
Havana.
  Havana who?
Havana go home!

Knock-Knock.
Who's there?
Hive.
Hive who?
Hive got a crush on you.

Knock-Knock.
Who's there?
Hopi.
Hopi who?
Hopi new year!

Knock-Knock.
Who's there?
Honeybee.
Honeybee who?
Honeybee nice and open the door.

Knock-Knock.
　Who's there?
Ice cream.
　Ice cream who?
Ice cream for you to open the door.

Knock-Knock.
　Who's there?
Ima.
　Ima who?
Ima waiting for you to come out and play.

Knock-Knock.
　Who's there?
Ilona.
　Ilona who?
Ilona you my bike — now give it back!

Knock-Knock.
   Who's there?
Jamaica.
   Jamaica who?
Jamaica fool of yourself again?

Knock-Knock.
   Who's there?
Joel.
   Joel who?
"Joel Macdonald had a farm."

Knock-Knock.
   Who's there?
Jimmy.
   Jimmy who?
Jimmy a raise in my allowance.

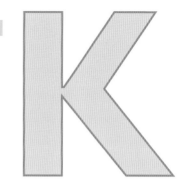

Knock-Knock.
   Who's there?
Kitten.
   Kitten who?
Kitten caboodle.

Knock-Knock.
   Who's there?
Kelp.
   Kelp who?
Kelp yourself to the French fries.

Knock-Knock.
   Who's there?
Kitchen, kitchen.
   Kitchen, kitchen who?
Don't do that, I'm ticklish.

L

Knock-Knock.
　Who's there?
Lena.
　Lena who?
Lena little closer and I'll tell you a secret.

Knock-Knock.
　Who's there?
Lass.
　Lass who?
Lass one home is a rotten egg.

Knock-Knock.
　Who's there?
Leif.
　Leif who?
Leif me alone.

Knock-Knock.
  Who's there?
Lionel.
  Lionel who?
Lionel roar if it's hungry.

Knock-Knock.
  Who's there?
Lux.
  Lux who?
Lux like rain. Let me in!

Knock-Knock.
  Who's there?
Llama.
  Llama who?
Llama bit lost. Can you point the way to the North Pole?

M

Knock-Knock.
  Who's there?
Maya.
  Maya who?
Maya big for your age.

Knock-Knock.
  Who's there?
Mischa.
  Mischa who?
Mischa since you've been away.

Knock-Knock.
  Who's there?
Mary Hannah.
  Mary Hannah who?
Mary Hannah little lamb.

Knock-Knock.
 Who's there?
Myer.
 Myer who?
Myer in a bad mood today.

Knock-Knock.
 Who's there?
Moose.
 Moose who?
Moose be something I ate.

Knock-Knock.
 Who's there?
Mustache.
 Mustache who?
Mustache — I'm in a hurry.

Knock-Knock.
   Who's there?
Needle.
   Needle who?
Needle the help I can get.

Knock-Knock.
   Who's there?
Never-Never Land.
   Never-Never Land who?
**Never-Never Land money
to a stranger.**

Knock-Knock.
   Who's there?
Noah.
   Noah who?
Noah-body here but me.

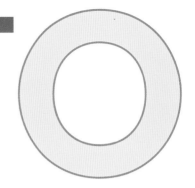

Knock-Knock.
　Who's there?
Omar.
　Omar who?
**Omar feet are sore. Can
I come in and rest?**

Knock-Knock.
　Who's there?
Oily.
　Oily who?
Oily to bed, oily to rise.

Knock-Knock.
　Who's there?
Omelet.
　Omelet who?
**Omelet smarter than
I look.**

Knock-Knock.
   Who's there?
Oprah.
   Oprah who?
Oprah the rainbow...

Knock-Knock.
   Who's there?
Orange.
   Orange who?
Orange you going to open the door?

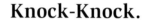

Knock-Knock.
   Who's there?
Owl.
   Owl who?
Owl be seeing you.

Knock-Knock.
   Who's there?
Otis.
   Otis who?
Otis is a great day for a picnic.

Knock-Knock.
　Who's there?
Papaya.
　Papaya who?
**Papaya the Sailor
Man.**

Knock-Knock.
　Who's there?
Panther.
　Panther who?
**Panther in the wash,
so I wore my shorts.**

Knock-Knock.
　Who's there?
Peephole.
　Peephole who?
Peephole say you're a nice guy.

Knock-Knock.
Who's there?
Police.
Police who?
Police don't talk about me when I'm gone.

Knock-Knock.
Who's there?
Pizza.
Pizza who?
Pizza that apple pie would be good.

Knock-Knock.
Who's there?
Pencil.
Pencil who?
Pencil fall down if you don't wear a belt.

Knock-Knock.
Who's there?
Quebec.
Quebec who?
Quebec to the drawing board.

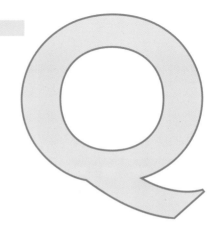

Knock-Knock.
Who's there?
Quiche.
Quiche who?
Quiche me, you fool!

Knock-Knock.
Who's there?
Queen.
Queen who?
Queen up your room.

Knock-Knock.
    Who's there?
Rough.
    Rough who?
**Rough. Rough. This is your
dog speaking...**

Knock-Knock.
    Who's there?
Raisin.
    Raisin who?
Raisin the roof!

Knock-Knock.
  Who's there?
Russia.
  Russia who?
Russia large pizza to this address.

Knock-Knock.
  Who's there?
Radio.
  Radio who?
Radio not, here I come!

Knock-Knock.
 Who's there?
Seymour.
 Seymour who?
Seymour of your friends if you'd open the door once in a while.

 Knock-Knock.
  Who's there?
 Sanitize.
  Sanitize who?
 Sanitize his reindeer to the sleigh.

 Knock-Knock.
  Who's there?
 Sahara.
  Sahara who?
 Sahara you today?

Knock-Knock.
　Who's there?
Sheila.
　Sheila who?
"Sheila be comin' round the mountain when she comes..."

Knock-Knock.
　Who's there?
Sir.
　Sir who?
Sir–PRIZE!

Knock-Knock.
　Who's there?
Snake.
　Snake who?
"Snake me out to the ball game..."

T

Knock-Knock.
   Who's there?
Tacoma.
   Tacoma who?
**Tacoma your hair —
it's a mess.**

Knock-Knock.
   Who's there?
Tamara.
   Tamara who?
Tamara is another day.

Knock-Knock.
   Who's there?
Taiwan.
   Taiwan who?
Taiwan to be happy.

Knock-Knock.
  Who's there?
Ticket.
  Ticket who?
Ticket or leave it.

Knock-Knock.
  Who's there?
Titan.
  Titan who?
Titan your seat belt!

Knock-Knock.
  Who's there?
Tom Sawyer.
  Tom Sawyer who?
Tom Sawyer underwear.

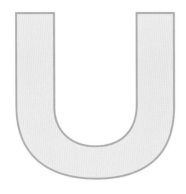

Knock-Knock.
   Who's there?
Utica.
   Utica who?
Utica words right out of my mouth.

Knock-Knock.
   Who's there?
U-Turn.
   U-turn who?
U-Turn off the doorbell?

Knock-Knock.
   Who's there?
Uniform.
   Uniform who?
Uniform a straight line and stand at attention.

Knock-Knock.
Who's there?
Viper.
Viper who?
Viper your hands, they're all wet.

Knock-Knock.
Who's there?
Viola.
Viola who?
**Viola fuss? I'm only
five minutes late.**

Knock-Knock.
Who's there?
Vera.
Vera who?
Vera the cupcakes?

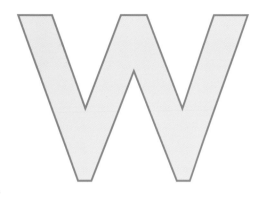

Knock-Knock.
  Who's there?
Wooden shoe.
  Wooden shoe who?
Wooden shoe like to go out for a walk?

Knock-Knock.
  Who's there?
Wilma.
  Wilma who?
Wilma parrot ever speak?

Knock-Knock.
  Who's there?
Window.
  Window who?
Window we eat?

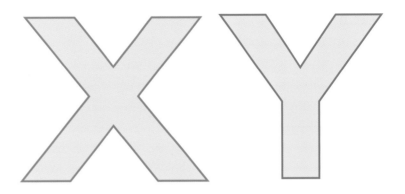

Knock-Knock.
   Who's there?
Xylophone.
   Xylophone who?
Xylophone and call me.

Knock-Knock.
   Who's there?
Yoda.
   Yoda who?
Yoda best!

Knock-Knock.
  Who's there?
Yuko.
  Yuko who?
Yuko your way, I'll go mine.

Knock-Knock.
  Who's there?
Yuma.
  Yuma who?
Yuma best friend.

Knock-Knock.
Who's there?
Zookeeper.
Zookeeper who?
Zookeeper your shirt on!

Knock-Knock.
Who's there?
Zenda.
Zenda who?
Zenda walls came tumbling down.

Knock-Knock.
Who's there?
Zys.
Zys who?
Zys is the end of the chapter!

How do you talk to a dinosaur?
Use big words.

Knock-Knock.
　Who's there?
Dozen.
　Dozen who?
Dozen anyone want to see my pet dinosaur?

What's as big as a dinosaur but weighs nothing?
A dinosaur's shadow.

Why did the dinosaur
sit on the bus?
**It was too big to sit
IN the bus.**

What would you have if a
dinosaur sat on your room?
A mush-room.

What did Humpty Dumpty do when a
dinosaur sat on him?
Called 911 on his shell phone.

What does a Triceratops sit on?
Its Tricera-bottom.

What vegetable do you get if a dinosaur
sits on your dinner plate?
Squash.

How would you feel if a dinosaur fell on you?
Very, very dino-sore.

Why don't dinosaurs have wings?
They like chicken nuggets better.

What do dinosaurs eat with their cheeseburgers?
Dragonfries.

What do you get if a dinosaur sits on your French fries?
Mashed potatoes.

What do dinosaurs eat on cruises?
Fish and ships.

On which day does a Tyrannosaurus eat people?
Chewsday.

Why does a Tyrannosaurus eat raw meat?
It never learned how to cook.

Why do dinosaurs eat snowmen?
They melt in the mouth.

What happens when a
dinosaur sneezes?
It blows your mind.

What direction does a
dinosaur sneeze travel?
Atchoo!

What should you do when a
dinosaur sneezes?
Get out of the way.

Why don't many dinosaurs celebrate their birthdays?
Two-hundred million candles won't fit on the cake.

Why don't dinosaurs ski?
No one sells size 3000 ski boots.

Why don't dinosaurs take ballet lessons?
They're just tutu big.

Where was the dinosaur when the sun went down?
In the dark.

What does a dinosaur get if it drops jam on its tummy?
A jellybutton.

What do you do if you find a sleepy dinosaur in your peanut butter sandwich?
Read it a breadtime story.

What do you call a
sleeping dinosaur?
A Stegosnorus.

What do dinosaurs
sleep on?
Bedrock.

How do you know there's a dinosaur
at your sleepover?
It has a D on its pajamas.

What do dinosaurs have that no other animals have?
Baby dinosaurs.

How would you find dinosaur eggs?
Go on an eggspedition.

What do baby dinosaurs use to get out of their eggs?
Hatch-ets.

What did the Stegosaurus use to build its dog house?
A dino-saw.

What's the best way to raise a dinosaur?
With a crane.

How fast did the dinosaur get back to its nest of eggs?
It scrambled.

What should you do if you find a dinosaur in your bathtub?
Pull out the plug!

How do dinosaurs bathe?
They take meteor showers.

How can you tell if there's a dinosaur in your shower?
You can't close the curtain.

Why do dinosaurs shower with mice?
So they'll be squeaky clean.

Why do dinosaurs take
showers?
To get ex-stinked.

What time does a
Tyrannosaurus get up?
Ate o'clock.

What would happen if a
dinosaur sat in front of you
at the theater?
**You'd miss the whole
movie!**

How can you tell if a
Tyrannosaurus has been
to the movies?
By the popcorn stuck in its teeth.

What should you do if a dinosaur burps
pepperoni breath in your face?
Give it a pizza your mind.

Why did the Tyrannosaurus go to school?

It heard the cafeteria was serving Baked Beings.

What does a Tyrannosaurus like eating most in the school cafeteria?

The lunch tables.

What's a dinosaur's favorite class?

Mashematics.

How did the little dinosaurs like their first day at preschool?

They had a bawl.

What time is it when ten dinosaurs chase you in your sleep?
    Ten after one.

How did the Velociraptor move so fast?
    It ran through quicksand.

Why can't we hide from a Tyrannosaurus?
    Because the dino saw us.

What's the fastest way to get to the hospital?
Pick a fight with a Velociraptor.

Why did the Apatosaurus cross the road?
Because the Tyrannosaurus ate the chicken.

What happens when dinosaurs run out of firecrackers?
They use dino-mite.

How can you tell if a dinosaur is a vegetarian?
Lie down on a plate.

Why does a Tyrannosaurus chase its prey?
It loves fast food.

What does a Tyrannosaurus call a car full of people?
A lunch box.

What does a Brachiosaurus eat every morning?
Brachfast.

Why can't dinosaurs keep secrets?
They have big mouths.

How do you ask a Tyrannosaurus to lunch?
"Tea, Rex?"

What treat do dinosaurs
make over a campfire?
Dino-s'mores.

What happened when the
Tyrannosaurus met the Apatosaurus?
It was love at first bite.

What game should you never play
with a dinosaur?
Leap frog.

Why couldn't the
dinosaur play games
on the computer?
**The Tyrannosaurus
ate the mouse.**

What's a dinosaur's
favorite dance?
The Stomp.

Where did the Tyrannosaurus go to dance?
To the Meat Ball.

How did the King's men find Cinderellasaurus
after the ball?
They followed her Foot Prince.

How do we know dinosaurs
flossed their teeth?
**Scientists found the
flossils.**

What does a Tyrannosaurus swear
in court?
**To tell "the tooth, the whole
tooth, and nothing but the
tooth."**

What's so great about
dinosaur teeth?
**They're totally
gnawsome.**

What time is it when a Tyrannosaurus
visits the dentist?
Tooth-hurty.

What happens when Tyrannosauruses
visit the dentist?
They're nervous rex.

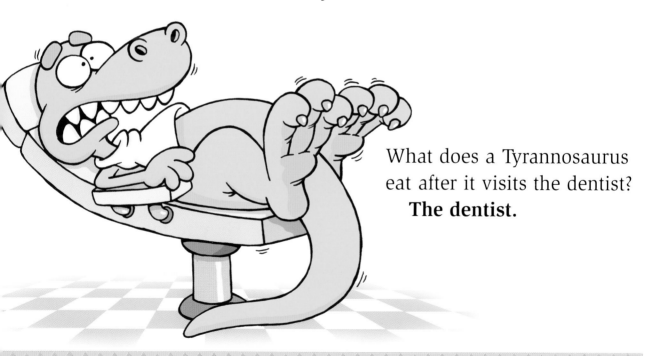

What does a Tyrannosaurus
eat after it visits the dentist?
The dentist.

What does a Tyrannosaurus do when it exercises?
Crunches.

Where can you find dinosaurs at the playground?
On the rock-slide.

How much do dinosaur bones weigh?
Skele-tons.

What size T-shirt do dinosaurs wear?
XXXXXXXXXXXXXX-Large.

What does an Apatosaurus wear to aerobics class?
Sweatplants.

Where does a Tyrannosaurus keep its sneakers?
In the bedroom claws-it.

What was the
Apatosaurus doing
on the highway?
**About two
miles per hour.**

Where does an Apatosaurus
fill up?
At the grass-station.

What does a Tyrannosaurus
say when introduced?
"Pleased to eat you."

What do you use to see distant dinosaurs?
Dinoculars.

Where do cows go to see dinosaur skeletons?
To moo-seums.

Which vegetable is helpful in finding dinosaur bones?
Clue-cumbers.

What do you call dinosaur skeletons lying on the ground?
Lazy bones.

What kind of dinosaurs live at the North Pole?
Cold ones!

What do you call a dinosaur at the South Pole?
Lost.

What's a T. Rex at the North Pole called?
Iced T.

Why doesn't Stegosaurus
play when it rains?
Because Stegosau-rust.

Who brings
Tyrannosaurus
presents on
Christmas Eve?
Santa Claws.

What do dinosaurs wear under
their raincoats?
Thunderwear.

Why can't dinosaurs go swimming?
The elephants have all the trunks.

What happens when a dinosaur
goes swimming?
It gets wet.

Do dinosaurs like going to
the beach?
They shore do.

What should you wear to Dinosaur Beach?
Sunscream.

Where do reptiles apply their sunscreen?
On their rep-tails.

What do you call a dinosaur on your pool chair?
The Big Dripper.

How would you feel if you saw real live dinosaurs?
Very, very old.

On which side does a Stegosaurus have the most scales?
The outside.

Why don't dinosaurs have antennae?
Because they get cable.

How big is a
dinosaur picnic?
Enormess.

How can you tell if a Stegosaurus is going
on a picnic?
By the plates on its back.

What happens when dinosaurs picnic
on top of volcanoes?
They have a blast.

Why don't dinosaurs drive convertibles?
Their heads bump the traffic lights.

How do you get a
Triceratops' attention?
Honk its horn.

What do you call a dinosaur
that never gives up?
Try-try-try-ceratops.

What happened when dinosaurs started driving?
They had Tyrannosaurus Wrecks.

Where do dinosaurs park their jeeps?
In Jurassic Parking lots.

How do dinosaurs fly from coast to coast?
On jumbo jets.

How can you tell if there's a dinosaur under your bed?
Your nose bumps the ceiling.

What does a dinosaur use to clean the kitchen floor?
Tricera-mops.

In what age did dinosaurs refuse to clean their rooms?
The Messy-zoic period.

What would you do if you found a dinosaur in your bed?
Sleep on the sofa.

Did you hear about the turkey dinosaur?
It gobbles you up.

What does a Tyrannosaurus eat at Sunday dinner?
Roast beast.

What do dinosaurs like to do at parties?
Crash them.

Why do dinosaurs have wrinkled skin?
They don't have time to iron.

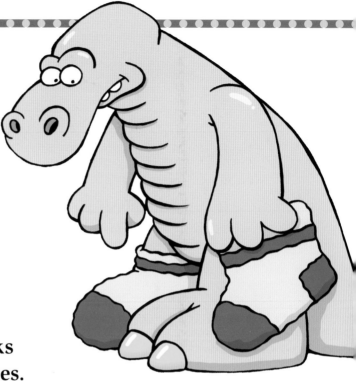

How do dinosaurs count to 2?
Take off their socks and count their toes.

Why did the dinosaur paint her toenails red?
So she could hide in the strawberry patch.

Why do dinosaurs' earrings keep falling off?
They don't have any earlobes.

Where does a Tyrannosaurus find its meat?
At the preyground.

What do dinosaurs
eat on their cactus
sandwiches?
   Dill prickles.

How do dinosaurs like
their chicken?
   Petrifried.

Which dinosaur knocks at your door?
The rap-rap-raptor!

What good is a dinosaur's snout?
It nose how to find you.

What do you have if a Tyrannosaurus gets mad at your cat?
A real cat-astrophe.

What's the difference between a dinosaur
and a flea?
About 50 tons.

How do dinosaurs fight?
With dino-swords.

Which dinosaur wears a
ten-gallon hat?
Tyrannosaurus Tex.

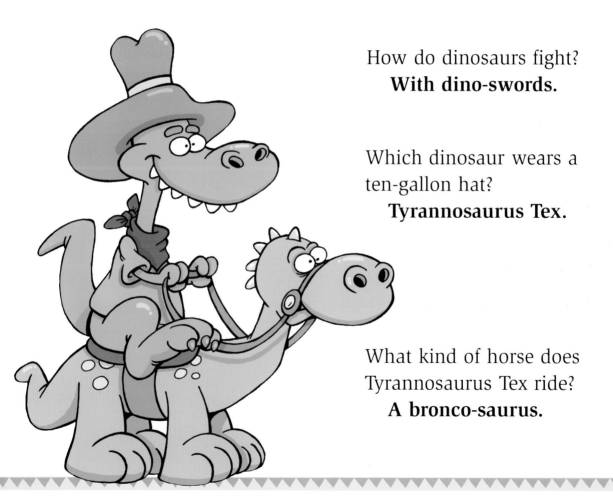

What kind of horse does
Tyrannosaurus Tex ride?
A bronco-saurus.

What is Dracula's favorite dinosaur?
The Terror-dactyl.

Who is Harry Pottersaurus?
The Lizard Wizard.

What's an Elvisaurus?
The King of the Dinosaurs.

What would you get if you crossed a dinosaur with a lemon?

A dinosour.

What would you get if you crossed a dinosaur with a skunk?

A Stinkosaurus.

Which dinosaurs sing and dance on MTV?

Rap-tors.

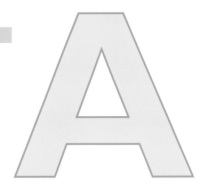

Arnie's oranges aren't as orange
as Arnold's oranges.

What ails Alex? asks Alice.
What ails Alex? asks Alice.
What ails Alex? asks Alice.

*How many times can you say
this in ten seconds?*
Alice asks for axes.

Apes ate Kate's cake.
Apes ate Kate's cake.
Apes ate Kate's cake.

B

Bernie's thirty dirty turtles.
Bernie's thirty dirty turtles.
Bernie's thirty dirty turtles.

A big bug hit a bold bald bear.
A big bug hit a bold bald bear.
A big bug hit a bold bald bear.

92

Brandy bandaged the bear.
Brandy bandaged the bear.
Brandy bandaged the bear.

Bad black bran bread.
Bad black bran bread.
Bad black bran bread.

A box of mixed biscuits
and a biscuit mixer.

Brenda Black was blameless.
Brenda Black was blameless.
Brenda Black was blameless.

How many times can you say this in ten seconds?
Big blue bubbles.

Bess's pet pestered Fess.
Bess's pet pestered Fess.
Bess's pet pestered Fess.

Byron's butler brought Byron's brother butter.
Byron's butler brought Byron's brother butter.
Byron's butler brought Byron's brother butter.

Bring the black boot back.
Bring the black boot back.
Bring the black boot back.

A cheeky chimp.
A cheeky chimp.
A cheeky chimp.

A canner exceedingly canny
One morning remarked to his granny,
"A canner can can
Anything that he can,
But a canner can't can a can, can he?"

How many times can you say this in ten seconds?
Chop suey shop.

Does this shop stock cheap checkers?
Does this shop stock cheap checkers?
Does this shop stock cheap checkers?

A cupcake cook in a cupcake cook's cap.
A cupcake cook in a cupcake cook's cap.
A cupcake cook in a cupcake cook's cap.

Chester chucked chestnuts.
Chester chucked chestnuts.
Chester chucked chestnuts.

How many times can you say this in ten seconds?

The drummers drummed and the strummers strummed.

Does a double bubble gum double bubble?
Does a double bubble gum double bubble?
Does a double bubble gum double bubble?

Dave's dogs dig deep ditches.
Dave's dogs dig deep ditches.
Dave's dogs dig deep ditches.

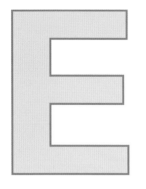

E

Eddie's enemies envied Eddie's energy.
Eddie's enemies envied Eddie's energy.
Eddie's enemies envied Eddie's energy.

Every errand Randy ran
for Erin was in error.

Eleven little leather loafers.
Eleven little leather loafers.
Eleven little leather loafers.

How many times can you say this in ten seconds?
Eight eager elephants.

Can a flying fish flee far from a free fish fry?
Can a flying fish flee far from a free fish fry?
Can a flying fish flee far from a free fish fry?

For fine fresh fish, phone Phil.
For fine fresh fish, phone Phil.
For fine fresh fish, phone Phil.

A fish sauce shop's
    sure to sell fresh
    fish sauce.
A fish sauce shop's
    sure to sell fresh
    fish sauce.
A fish sauce shop's
    sure to sell fresh
    fish sauce.

Friendly fleas and
    fireflies.
Friendly fleas and
    fireflies.
Friendly fleas and
    fireflies.

Friendly fleas and huffy fruit flies.
Friendly fleas and huffy fruit flies.
Friendly fleas and huffy fruit flies.

How many times can you say this in ten seconds?
French shrimp shop.

Fifty-five flags flutter freely.
Fifty-five flags flutter freely.
Fifty-five flags flutter freely.

A fat-free fruit float.
A fat-free fruit float.
A fat-free fruit float.

How many times can you say this in ten seconds?
Free flag.

How many times can you say this in ten seconds?
Grape cakes.

Gus goes by Blue Goose bus.
Gus goes by Blue Goose bus.
Gus goes by Blue Goose bus.

The cruel ghoul cooks gruel.
The cruel ghoul cooks gruel.
The cruel ghoul cooks gruel.

How many times can you say this in ten seconds?
Gabby gray gobblers.

Great gray geese graze.
Great gray geese graze.
Great gray geese graze.

The grave groom grew glum.
The grave groom grew glum.
The grave groom grew glum.

H

Hillary's hairy hound hardly hurries.
Hillary's hairy hound hardly hurries.
Hillary's hairy hound hardly hurries.

How many times can you say this in ten seconds?

Heed the head henpecker!

The hairy hare stares
at the hairier hare.
The hairy hare stares
at the hairier hare.
The hairy hare stares
at the hairier hare.

Imagine managing an imaginary menagerie.
Imagine managing an imaginary menagerie.
Imagine managing an imaginary menagerie.

I'll lie idle on the isle.
I'll lie idle on the isle.
I'll lie idle on the isle.

How many time can you say this in ten seconds?

Six sick insects.

Jill's giraffe juggled
 jam jars.
Jill's giraffe juggled
 jam jars.
Jill's giraffe juggled
 jam jars.

*How many times can you say
this in ten seconds?*
 Just dust.

Jack's giraffe juggled jelly jars.
Jack's giraffe juggled jelly jars.
Jack's giraffe juggled jelly jars.

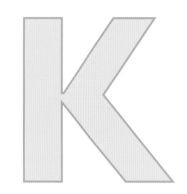

Keep clean socks in a clean sock stack.
Keep clean socks in a clean sock stack.
Keep clean socks in a clean sock stack.

Knee deep, deep knee.
Knee deep, deep knee.
Knee deep, deep knee.

How many times can you say this in ten seconds?
    A knapsack strap.

King Kong plays Ping Pong.
King Kong plays Ping Pong.
King Kong plays Ping Pong.

L

A lump of red leather, a red leather lump.
A lump of red leather, a red leather lump.
A lump of red leather, a red leather lump.

Ladylike lowland llamas.
Ladylike lowland llamas.
Ladylike lowland llamas.

Larry's lair lacks locks.
Larry's lair lacks locks.
Larry's lair lacks locks.

How many times can you say this in ten seconds?
Lemon-lime liniment.

Lee loves to rob lobsters.
Lee loves to rob lobsters.
Lee loves to rob lobsters.

Local loggers' lawyers.
Local loggers' lawyers.
Local loggers' lawyers.

M

I miss my Swiss Miss and my Swiss Miss misses me.
I miss my Swiss Miss and my Swiss Miss misses me.
I miss my Swiss Miss and my Swiss Miss misses me.

Monster mother's muffins.
Monster mother's muffins.
Monster mother's muffins.

Much mushroom mash.
Much mushroom mash.
Much mushroom mash.

How many times can you say this in ten seconds?
Matt's mismatched mittens.

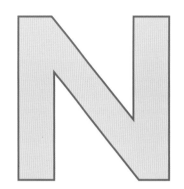

How many times can you say this in ten seconds?

Nine nimble noblemen.

Ninety-nine knitted knickknacks
were nicked by ninety-nine knitted knickknack nickers.

I need not your needles,
They're needless to me,
For the needing of needles
Is needless, you see.
But did my neat trousers
But need to be kneed,
I then should have need
Of your needles indeed.

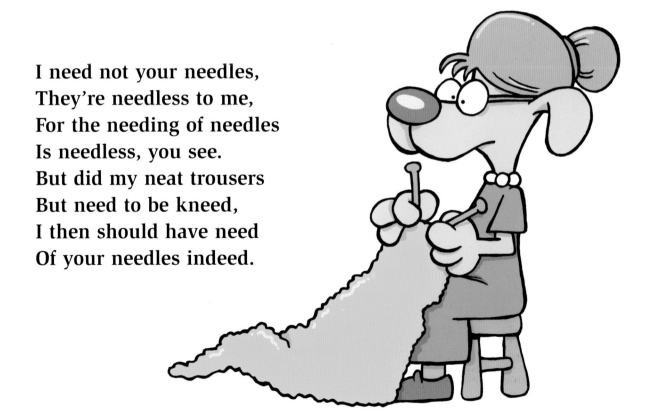

Ollie oils oily autos.
Ollie oils oily autos.
Ollie oils oily autos.

How many times can you say this in ten seconds?
One worm wiggled.

Orville ordered ordinary ornaments.
Orville ordered ordinary ornaments.
Orville ordered ordinary ornaments.

How many times can you say this in ten seconds?

Pass the pink peas please.

Please prune plum trees promptly.
Please prune plum trees promptly.
Please prune plum trees promptly.

The parrot pecked the pirate's pet.
The parrot pecked the pirate's pet.
The parrot pecked the pirate's pet.

Polly placed a plate of pasta
on Peter's pizza parlor poster.

A peck of pesky pixies.
A peck of pesky pixies.
A peck of pesky pixies.

Pat pet Peg's pig.
Pat pet Peg's pig.
Pat pet Peg's pig.

How many times can you say this in ten seconds?

Polly planted potted plants.

Poor pure Pierre.
Poor pure Pierre.
Poor pure Pierre.

People pay pros for playing.
People pay pros for playing.
People pay pros for playing.

Pretty precious plants.
Pretty precious plants.
Pretty precious plants.

Pretty promising peace prospects.
Pretty promising peace prospects.
Pretty promising peace prospects.

How many times can you say this in ten seconds?
Is a pleasant peasant's pheasant present?

Pale pink plumage.
Pale pink plumage.
Pale pink plumage.

The quack quit asking questions.
The quack quit asking questions.
The quack quit asking questions.

The queen coined quick quips.
The queen coined quick quips.
The queen coined quick quips.

Quakes cause cracks.
Quakes cause cracks.
Quakes cause cracks.

Russ was the wristwatch rust remover.
Russ was the wristwatch rust remover.
Russ was the wristwatch rust remover.

Rex wrecks wet rocks.
Rex wrecks wet rocks.
Rex wrecks wet rocks.

Wanda raised white roses.
Wanda raised white roses.
Wanda raised white roses.

*How many times can you say this
in ten seconds?*

Rush the washing, Russell.

**Real rear wheels.
Real rear wheels.
Real rear wheels.**

Round and round the rugged rocks the ragged rascal ran.

**The right fruit is ripe fruit.
The right fruit is ripe fruit.
The right fruit is ripe fruit.**

S

No shipshape ship's shop
stocks shop-soiled shirts.

*How many times can you say
this in ten seconds?*
Slick silk socks.

Seth's sharp spacesuit shrank.
Seth's sharp spacesuit shrank.
Seth's sharp spacesuit shrank.

The spunky skunk and the stinky slug.
The spunky skunk and the stinky slug.
The spunky skunk and the stinky slug.

Sixteen sloppy, smelly slippers.
Sixteen sloppy, smelly slippers.
Sixteen sloppy, smelly slippers.

How many times can you say this in ten seconds?
Six crisp snacks.

Is Sherry's shortcake shop shut?
Is Sherry's shortcake shop shut?
Is Sherry's shortcake shop shut?

*How many times can you say this
in ten seconds?*
Soft smooth snake skin.

**How many slim, slimy snakes
would slither silently to the sea,
If slim, slimy snakes
could slither silently?**

**Smart, small snakes smell thick smoked steaks.
Smart, small snakes smell thick smoked steaks.
Smart, small snakes smell thick smoked steaks.**

Sharp sharkskin shoes.
Sharp sharkskin shoes.
Sharp sharkskin shoes.

Sixty-six sticky skeletons.
Sixty-six sticky skeletons.
Sixty-six sticky skeletons.

How many times can you say this in ten seconds?
   Sad skunk.

Sloppy skiers slide on slick ski slopes.

How many times can you say this in ten seconds?

Such a shapeless sash!

Scams, stings, and skulduggery.
Scams, stings, and skulduggery.
Scams, stings, and skulduggery.

Mr. Spink thinks the Sphinx stinks.
Mr. Spink thinks the Sphinx stinks.
Mr. Spink thinks the Sphinx stinks.

Thick ticks think thin ticks are sick.
Thick ticks think thin ticks are sick.
Thick ticks think thin ticks are sick.

How many times can you say this in ten seconds?
Theo saw three sly thrushes.

Tea for the thin twin tinsmith!
Tea for the thin twin tinsmith!
Tea for the thin twin tinsmith!

There goes one tough top cop.
There goes one tough top cop.
There goes one tough top cop.

Unsung songs.
Unsung songs.
Unsung songs.

Vicious visitors vexed the village.
Vicious visitors vexed the village.
Vicious visitors vexed the village.

The wretched witch watched a walrus washing.
Did the wretched witch watch a walrus washing?
If the wretched witch watched a walrus washing,
Where's the washing walrus the wretched witch watched?

If two witches watched two watches,
Which witch would watch which watch?

How many times can you say this in ten seconds?

Which wristwatch is a Swiss wristwatch?

I wish I hadn't washed this wristwatch.
I washed all the wheels and the works.
Since this wristwatch got all washed,
Oh, how it jumps and jerks!

Wyatt wondered why the worn wires weren't
   wrapped right.
Wyatt wondered why the worn wires weren't
   wrapped right.
Wyatt wondered why the worn wires weren't
   wrapped right.

Wild wrens wing westward.
Wild wrens wing westward.
Wild wrens wing westward.

How many times can you say this in ten seconds?

One really wet red whale.

Wee Willie Winkie risks three wishes.
Wee Willie Winkie risks three wishes.
Wee Willie Winkie risks three wishes.

Weary railroad workers.
Weary railroad workers.
Weary railroad workers.

Agnes's X's are excellent.
Agnes's X's are excellent.
Agnes's X's are excellent.

Yesterday Yuri yelled at Euwell.
Usually, Euwell yells at Yuri.

The ex-egg-examiner.
The ex-egg-examiner.
The ex-egg-examiner.

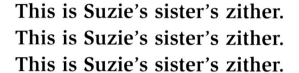

This is Suzie's sister's zither.
This is Suzie's sister's zither.
This is Suzie's sister's zither.

Zithers slither slowly south.
Zithers slither slowly south.
Zithers slither slowly south.

How many times can you say this in ten seconds?
Zack's backpack.

What has no fingers
but many rings?
A tree.

What kind of trees do fingers
grow on?
Palm trees.

What kind of tree keeps you warm?
A fir tree.

Why did the tree surgeon buy
another office?
He was branching out.

Why was the opera singer kicked out of class?
For passing notes.

What did the compact disk player say to the CD?
"Want to go for a spin?"

Why are pianos so hard to open?
The keys are inside.

What's a ghost's favorite kind of music?
Rhythm and boos.

Lonnie has it first. Phil has it last. Girls have it once.
Boys never have it. What is it?
The letter "L."

What did the pencil sharpener say to the pencil?
"Stop going around in circles and get to the point."

What is black and white and sleeps
all day?
A snooze paper.

What is lighter than a feather, but
can't be held for five minutes?
Your breath.

What do monsters eat for breakfast?

Screambled eggs.

What is the monsters' favorite play?

Romeo and Ghoul-iet.

HOMER: Did you hear about the monster with five legs?

GOMER: No, but I bet his pants fit him like a glove.

Where do baby monsters go when their parents are at work?
Day scare centers.

Who made the monster's wish come true?
His scary godmother.

DAD: Well, son, now that we got you a
waterbed, will you be able to sleep better?
SON: No, I'm afraid of sharks.

What did Godzilla eat when he arrived in New York?
The Big Apple.

What's Godzilla's favorite big sandwich?
Peanut butter and deli.

Why did the police give Godzilla a ticket?
He ran through a stomp sign.

How do kangaroos travel?
They jump ship.

How do chickens travel?
They fly the coop.

How do frogs travel?
They hop a plane.

What would you get if you arrested a chicken and a robber?

A peck-pocket.

What bug arrests other bugs?

A cop-roach.

How do you prevent break-ins at a diner?

With a burger alarm.

TEACHER: Billy, please use the word "arrest" in a sentence.

BILLY: After peddling my bike up a steep hill, I sure needed arrest.

JUDGE: The charge is stealing a blanket. How do you plead?
CROOK: Not quilty.

PRISON WARDEN: How would you like to celebrate
your birthday?
PRISONER: What would you think of an open house?

What did the thumbtack say
to the bulletin board?
"This is a stickup!"

Where do they put tomatoes
who break the law?
Behind salad bars.

What is a mummy's favorite treat?
Cotton candy.

What kind of underwear do mummies wear?
Fruit of the Tomb.

What did King Tut get for his birthday?
Gift wrap.

What did the traffic light say to the Martian?
"Don't look now — I'm changing."

What did the Martian say when he landed in a flower bed?
"Take me to your weeder."

How can you tell that Martians are good gardeners?
They have little green thumbs.

What photos do Arctic bears
keep in their scrapbooks?
Polaroids.

Why did the Abominable
Snowman miss a day of school?
He had a bad cold.

Where do penguins keep their money?
In snow banks.

What was the first thing the lumberjack did when he bought a computer?
He logged on.

What's the difference between a boxer and a computer program?
One's a bruiser; the other's a browser.

What did the computer say when the little lamb logged on?
"Ewe got mail."

What position did the Invisible
Man play on the baseball team?
No one knows.

What socks do baseball players like?
Ones with lots of runs in them.

What can you serve but never eat?
A volleyball.

How is an old comb like a hockey player?
They're both missing a few teeth.

Why don't elephants play football?
Their ears won't fit into the helmet.

What do you call a
football player who
keeps giving up?
A quitter-back.

How do rabbits stay in shape?

They do hare-robics.

Why was the swimming instructor fired?

He kept people wading too long.

What did the swimming pool say to the springboard?

"You're diving me crazy!"

What's the difference between a good sport and an umpire?

One plays by the rules and the other rules on the plays.

What's the difference between a cowboy and a locomotive driver?

One trains the steers, the other steers the trains.

What's the difference between a kid who collects insects and a cranky umpire?

One catches bugs, the other bugs catchers.

What kind of snakes are useful in your car?
Windshield vipers.

What kind of cars do rubber bands drive?
Stretch limos.

How do otters get around when the river dries up?
They drive otter-mobiles.

What's a hotdog's favorite car?
A Rolls.

What do zebras earn when they do their homework?
Stars and stripes.

How do babies get to school?
On a drool bus.

Why was the snake late for school?
It hissed the bus.

LENNY: I can't figure out this math problem.
TEACHER: Really? Any five-year-old should be able to solve it.
LENNY: No wonder. I'm nearly eight.

TEACHER: Cindy, would you take a note to your mother?
CINDY: Sure, how about a B-flat?

CAT: How are the mice doing in school?
TEACHER: They're barely squeaking by.

ZOOKEEPER: How are my apes doing in school?
TEACHER: They're always monkeying around.

FARMER: How are my cows doing in school?
TEACHER: They're copying off each udder.

GIANT SQUID: How are my little squids doing in school?
TEACHER: They can't ink straight yet.

MOTHER SQUIRREL: How are my little squirrels doing in school?
TEACHER: They're driving their teachers nuts.

GRANDMA TURTLE: How are the little turtles doing in school?
TEACHER: They're always late to class.

FATHER: How are the little parrots doing in school?
TEACHER: They've been talking all through study hall.

What is the first thing you say when you enter a haunted house?
Who ghost there?

What would you get if you crossed a ghoul with a cow?
Ghost beef.

What do ghosts play on rainy days?
Moan-o-poly.

What's a ghost's favorite dessert?
Cookies and scream.

Why was the Invisible Man heartbroken?
His girlfriend told him she couldn't see him anymore.

What werewolf came to visit Cinderella?
Her hairy godmother.

What do witches say when they cast the wrong spell?
"Hexcuse me!"

Why do gnomes carry plenty of spare change?
For the troll booth.

What did the frog drink when he went on a diet?
Diet Croak.

If you eat lady fingers with your hands, what do you eat with your feet?
Tofu.

What would you get if you crossed a lion with fruit and milk?
A man-eating smoothie.

What do plumbers eat for breakfast?
Wrench toast.

What's long and orange and flies at the speed of sound?
  A jet-propelled carrot.

What did the skeleton order at the restaurant?
  Spare ribs.

What do cows like on their toast?
  Mar-mooo-lade.

FOOD INSPECTOR: I'm afraid you have too many bugs in here.
RESTAURANT OWNER: How many am I allowed?

CUSTOMER: Waiter, what is this fly doing in my hamburger?
WAITER: Looks like the cha-cha-cha.

CUSTOMER: Waiter, does your chef have chicken legs?
WAITER: I don't know — I can't see under his apron.

How do flight attendants like their eggs?

Plane.

How do kids who are taking tests like their eggs?

Over easy.

How do weatherpersons like their eggs?

Sunny side up.

Did you hear about the strongest man in the circus? He could lift an elephant with one finger, but it took him ten years to find an elephant with one finger.

What's the difference between a fly and an elephant?
You can't zip an elephant.

What's big and gray and goes up and down, up and down?
An elephant on a pogo stick.

How can you tell the age of an elephant?

Count the candles on its birthday cake.

Why do elephants use their trunks to eat?
So their legs are free to tap dance.

POLICE *(to bank teller):* You say it was an elephant that robbed the bank?
BANK TELLER: Well, I can't be sure.
POLICE: Why is that?
BANK TELLER: It had a stocking on its head.

Did you hear about the man who had a heart transplant from a sheep? When the doctor asked how he felt, the patient said, "Not baaaaad!"

PATIENT: Yesterday I thought I was a pig.
DOCTOR: How are you today?
PATIENT: Swine, thanks.

What do you call a surgeon with 8 arms?
A doc-topus.

NIT: This ointment is making my legs smart.
WIT: Quick, rub some on your head!

WILL: My sister swallowed
    a watch.
BILL: Does it hurt?
WILL: Only when she tries
    to wind it.

What do you give a cowboy
with a cold?
   Cough stirrup.

Where do hornets go when they're sick?
The waspital.

Where do boats go when they're sick?
To the dock-tor.

Mother: Has your bad tooth stopped aching?
Bobby: I don't know. The dentist kept it.

Why did the mosquito go to the dentist?
To improve his bite.

What do dentists like to ride
at the amusement park?
The molar coaster.

What would you get if you crossed
a dentist with a weasel?
The Tooth Ferret.

PATIENT: Doctor, doctor, I think I'm a pretzel.

DOCTOR: I'll straighten you out in no time.

PATIENT: Doctor, doctor, everyone thinks I'm a liar.

DOCTOR: I find that hard to believe.

PATIENT: Doctor, Doctor, I think I'm a cow.

DOCTOR: Just open your mouth and say moo.

What's black and white and sleeps all day?
  A z-z-z-z-zebra.

What's black and white and blue all over?
  A zebra holding its breath.

What has black and white stripes on the inside and the outside?
  A zebra in prison.

What is black and white, black and white, and green?
  Two zebras fighting over a pickle.

MAY: I think I can put this wallpaper on myself.

RAY: Well, go ahead, but I think it would look better on the wall.

What would you get if you crossed boomerangs with bad Christmas presents?

Gifts that return themselves.

CUSTOMER: May I have a pair of alligator shoes?

SALESPERSON: Certainly. What size is your alligator?

Why did the pelican refuse to pay for its meal?

Its bill was too big.

What bird lives in a bakery?

A cream puffin.

Where do eagles do most of their shopping?

At the swoopermarket.

If a gull that lives near the ocean is called a seagull, what do you call a gull that lives near a bakery?

A bay-gull.

Why do chickens stay out of the sun?
**To keep from
getting fried.**

On what day do
spiders eat the most?
Flyday.

What goes beep-beep-beep, buck-buck-buck?
A chicken at an automatic teller machine.

Did you hear about the silkworm who became a story teller?
She just sits around all day and spins yarns.

What did the boy do when his pet rodent used bad words?
He washed his mouse out with soap.

Why did the sick skunk stay in bed for a week?
Doctors odors.

What would you call ten monkeys stuck on an island?
Chimp-wrecked.

How did the skunk call home?
It used its smell phone.

What position did the skunk play on the baseball team?
Scent-er field.

What do cats put on
after a bath?
Purr-fume.

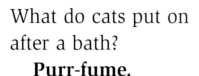

What do cats read to keep up
on current events?
The Evening Mews.

What did the cat major in at the police academy?
Claw Enforcement.

What would you get if you crossed a cat and a porcupine?
An animal that goes "meowch" whenever it licks itself.

Index